From the desktops of Andy and Gil Leaf

One of the most important lessons our father taught us—above good manners—is the value of reading. The exhilaration of turning a page and having words leap out, begging to be uttered and embraced, is a profound experience that is permanently etched in the mind. This was his message to every child. 'A springboard for the imagination, a book can be educational *and* fun.

It is a huge joy that the key to the amusing, creative, and engaging world of our father can once again be found on bookshelves. He would be tremendously pleased and satisfied to know that today, nearly seventy years and one century later, his words still have resonance—words that will be fondly remembered by generations past, and words that will be savored, chuckled over, and read countless times by a new generation of curious, inquisitive, and impressionable young eyes.

Your Name Here

MANNERS
CAN BE
FUN

First published in the United States of America in 2004
by UNIVERSE PUBLISHING
A Division of Rizzoli International Publications, Inc.
300 Park Avenue South
New York, NY 10010
www.rizzoliusa.com

2008 2009 2010 / 13 12 11 10

Printed in China

ISBN-13: 978-0-7893-1061-3

Library of Congress Catalog Control Number: 2003114671

Cover design: Headcase Design
www.headcasedesign.com

MANNERS CAN BE FUN

Munro Leaf

UNIVERSE

Having good manners is really just living with other people pleasantly.

If you lived all by
yourself

out on a desert island, others would not care whether you had good manners or not.

It wouldn't bother
them.

But if someone else lived there with you, you would both have to learn to get along together pleasantly. If you did not, you would probably quarrel and fight

all the time

or——

stay apart and be lonesome

because you could not have

a good time together.

Neither would be

much fun.

Most of us don't live

on desert islands

So this is

what

we

do—

WE
MEET PEOPLE

HOW DO YOU DO?

If I am a boy,

when I meet you for

the first time I smile

and shake your hand.

If you are a lady

or a girl

I take my hat off.

HOW DO YOU DO?

If I am a girl,

when I meet you for the
first time I smile and
hold out my hand to you.
I don't just stand

with my mouth open
and leave you holding
out *your* hand.

If we already

know you

we say

Good morning

or

Good afternoon

or

Good evening.

Very often the people we like most live in the same house with us.

We see them so often we sometimes forget to be as nice to them as we are to others.

Most of the time it is just because we do not think of it, so let's see how we start the day.

We get up

in

the morning

when we should

and we don't
have to be called

more than once.

We wash ourselves

and brush

our teeth

without fussing

and

making

faces.

And we don't leave our

clothes and towels around

for others to pick up.

When we are at

a good time

we eat what we

about pleasant things

the table we have

because

should and talk

we have seen and done.

We don't have

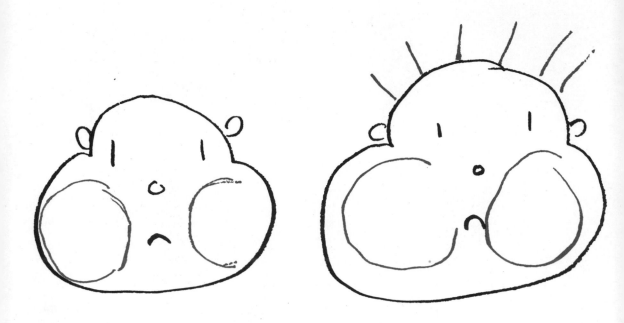

Puffy Cheeks

from talking with our

mouths full.

And we don't
CHOKE

because we don't drink
when we still have
food in our mouths.

Other people like to
talk to us because

 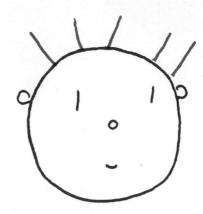

we wait until they finish
talking before we start.
We don't try to shout
louder and butt in

 like

goats.

If we want something

we

say

PLEASE

We say THANK YOU
if you help us or
give us something or
do things for us.

Before we leave the table

we ask if

we

may

be

excused.

And say 😊 THANK YOU 😊

if we are told we may.

PLAYING

When I play
with other boys

we take turns doing the things
we want to do.

If we are playing games we
follow the rules.

One of us doesn't always
try to change things so that
he will win.

We play for fun.

When I play

with other

girls

we share our things and take
turns doing what we like to most.

We don't whine and cry or
quarrel when we don't have

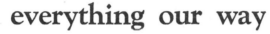

everything our way

and

go

home

angry.

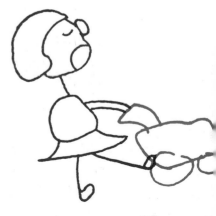

There are some
people we don't
like to play with
and here they are

THE PIGS

They have all sorts of toys but they never let anyone else play with them.

They just squeal
THAT'S MINE

This is a
WHINEY

Whineys always have lumps in their throats and cry because they can't do just what they want to.

 They whine if they can't have things they should not.

They whine if they can't go along when they should not

and they whine when other people tell them, No.

 OH, How They Whine.

THE NOISEYS

They shout and scream
and yell

until I can't even think.
They make so much

N O I S E

they make me tired

This is a ME FIRST

who never took turns.

He wore his arms off grabbing things first. He wore his legs off pushing in every place first and his face is this way because he always tried to see first.

S M A S H ⁘ R I P ⁘ R U I N

SMASH is never happy unless he is breaking things—his things—your things—everybody's things.

RIP is terrible. She destroys everything that she can tear. Books, dresses, paper—everything.

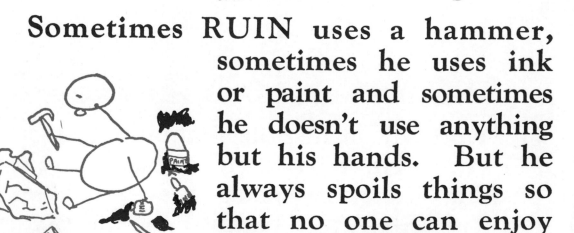

Sometimes RUIN uses a hammer, sometimes he uses ink or paint and sometimes he doesn't use anything but his hands. But he always spoils things so that no one can enjoy them any more.

PUTTING THINGS BACK

SMASH, RIP and RUIN nearly always destroy the things they use.

If they don't they forget to put them back where they belong.

Then other people come along and step on them or have to put things back for them.

Don't be a
SMASH
RIP
or
RUIN.

BE

KIND

TO

ANIMALS

THEY

HAVE

FEELINGS

TOO

39

VISITING

When we go to
visit someone and
have a good
time

we THANK them when
we leave and say
GOODBYE.

While we are there we do not act like

THE NOISEYS

THE PIGS

ME FIRST

WHINEYS

SMASH

RIP

RUIN

or

TOUCHEY and THE SNOOPERS

THIS
IS
TOUCHEY

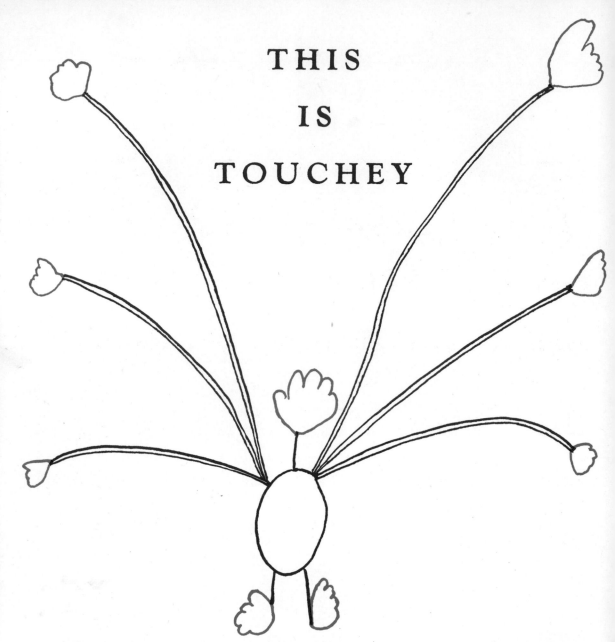

Wherever he goes he touches things.
He never thinks whether he should
or not— Maybe it's because
he hasn't any head—he is all hands.

SNOOPERS

walk

right

into rooms

where other people are

when the doors are closed.

If they knocked first

and asked if they might

come in,

people

would not

call them

SNOOPERS.

THIS IS YAWNER

who yawned so much without putting his hand over his mouth that his mouth grew too big to cover.   SO SAD.

WHEN
NIGHT
COMES

It is time for sleep

and people who
like us all
the day

Say GOODNIGHT.

Then it is time

for us

to

go.

Only WHINEYS

stand about

while we

are first

in—

BED

THESE NEXT PAGES

ARE ABOUT OTHER

MANNERS THAT

I HAVE LEARNED

AND

THE

PICTURES

ARE

DRAWN

BY